LEARN TO DRAW

AMERICAN LANDMARKS
& HISTORICAL HEROES

Illustrated by Maury Aaseng • Written by Stephanie Meissner

TABLE OF CONTENTS

INTRODUCTION

From sea to shining sea, the United States of America is brimming with history, natural beauty, and iconic people and places.

In 1776, fifty-six men—including future presidents John Adams and Thomas Jefferson—signed the Declaration of Independence, thereby freeing the original 13 colonies from Britain's rule. A year later, the Revolutionary War began, and on October 19, 1781, America won its independence when Britain surrendered. What began as 13 small colonies eventually grew to 50 states. The U.S.A. is now the third largest country in the world!

Follow along as we explore this great land—from coast to coast, mountains to plains, and fields to deserts. Along the way, you'll learn how to draw some of America's renowned people and historical places, as well as symbols and features that make each state unique.

Turn the page to get started in your drawing journey across America!

Tools & Materials

Before you get started, gather some drawing tools, such as paper, a regular pencil, an eraser, a pencil sharpener, and a ruler. For color you can use colored pencils, crayons, markers, or even paint!

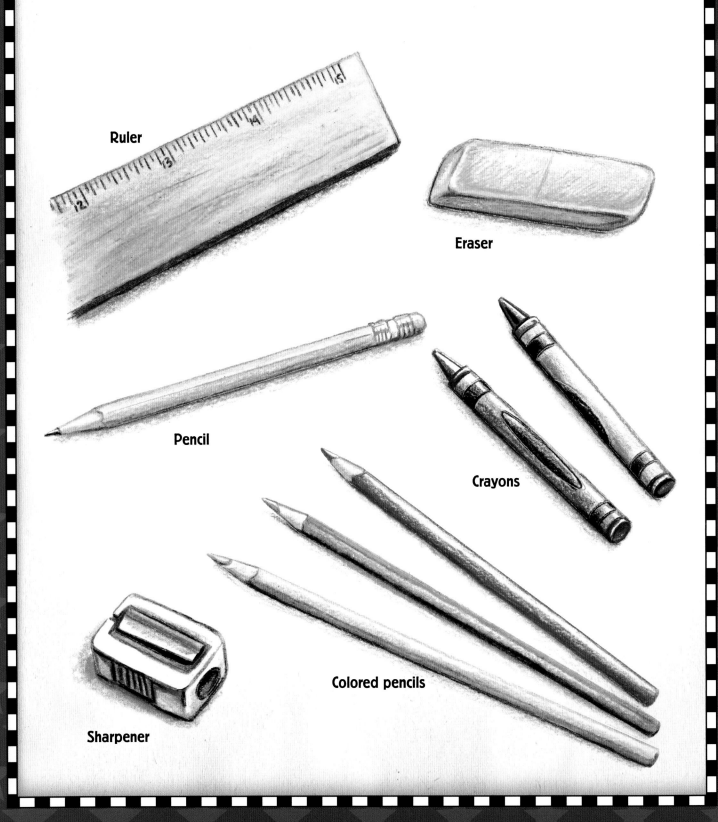

Ruler

Eraser

Pencil

Crayons

Colored pencils

Sharpener

Drawing Exercises

Before you begin, warm up your hand by drawing different kinds of squiggles and lines.

As you start to draw the projects in this book, you'll notice that they're made up of basic shapes, such as circles, triangles, and rectangles. With a few basic shapes, you can draw just about anything. Check it out!

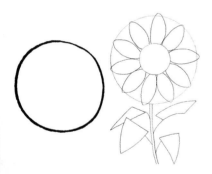

Circles are good for drawing flowers or heads.

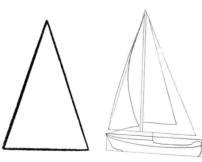

Triangles are good for drawing sails and leaves.

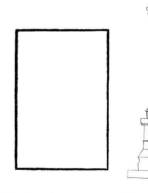

Rectangles are good for drawing statues and monuments.

Ovals are good for drawing birds and animals.

Squares are good for drawing buildings.

DELAWARE

1ST STATE

The coat of arms on Delaware's state flag represents shipping, farming, hunting, and cattle ranching.

STATE FLAG

1

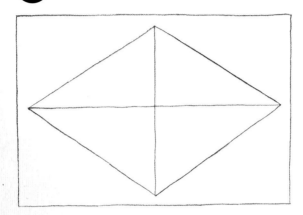

2

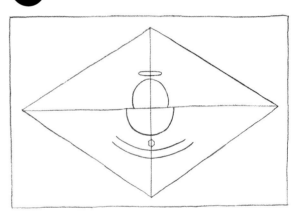

3

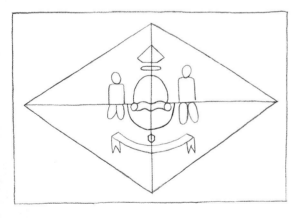

4

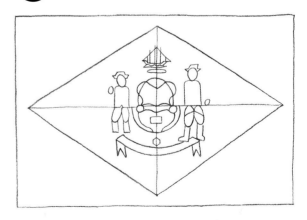

DOVER

5

6

7

8

STATE FACT

Delaware was the first state to ratify, or approve, the Constitution, earning the nickname The First State.

PENNSYLVANIA

2ND STATE

Independence Hall and the Liberty Bell are both iconic symbols of freedom. The Declaration of Independence was signed at Independence Hall in 1776.

INDEPENDENCE HALL

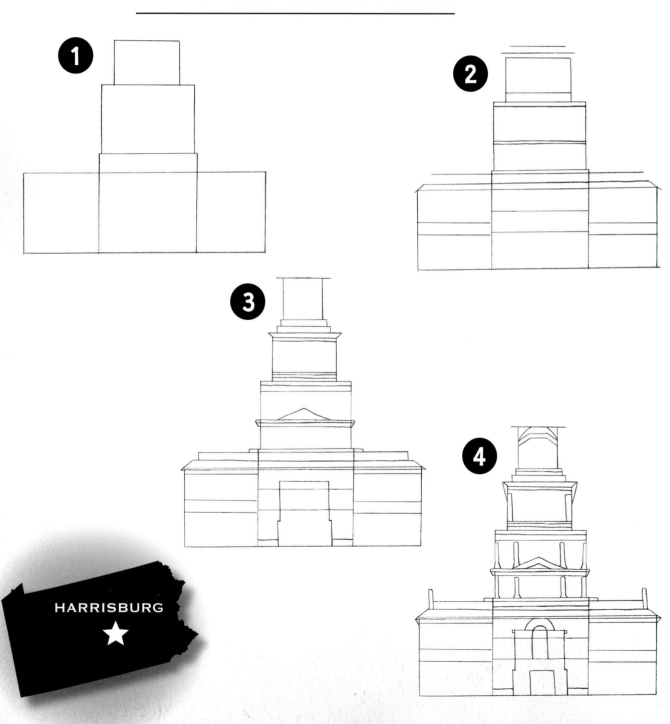

HARRISBURG ★

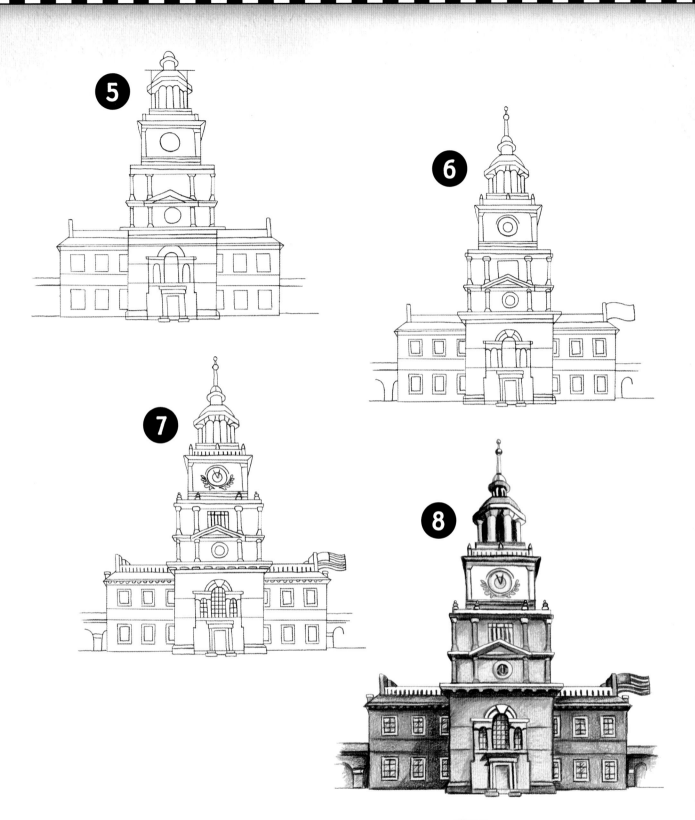

5

6

7

8

STATE FACT

Independence Hall is featured on the back of the $100 bill.

LIBERTY BELL

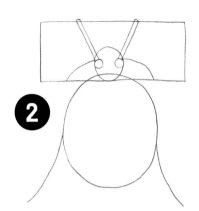

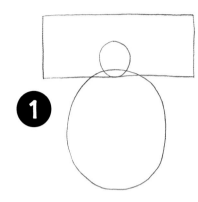

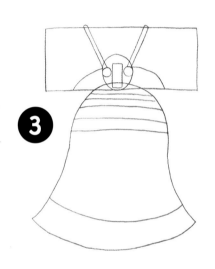

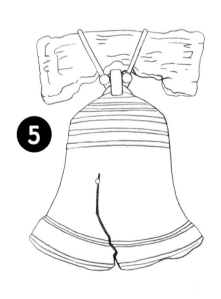

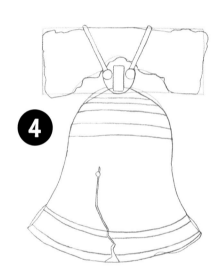

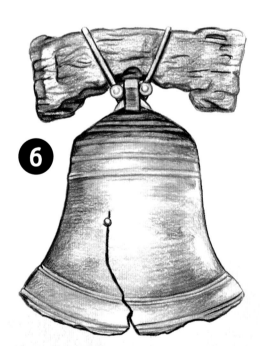

GEORGIA

4TH STATE

**Known as The Peach State, Georgia hosts
a peach festival every year in Peach County.**

PEACH

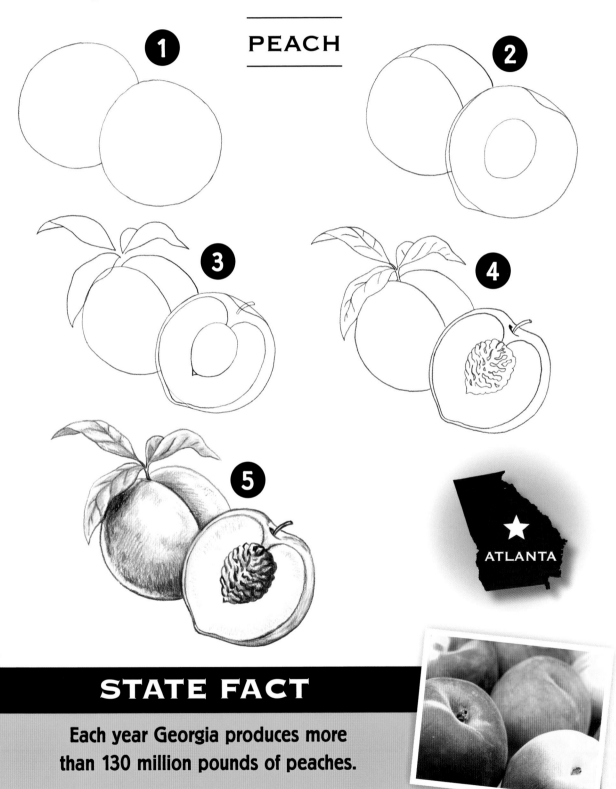

1

2

3

4

5

ATLANTA

STATE FACT

**Each year Georgia produces more
than 130 million pounds of peaches.**

NEW JERSEY

3RD STATE

General George Washington and the Continental army spent nearly half of the Revolutionary War in New Jersey.

REVOLUTIONARY WAR SOLDIER

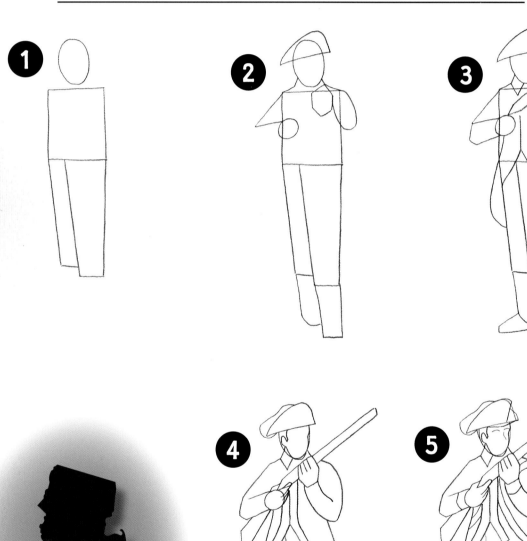

TRENTON

STATE FACT

New Jersey militia played an important role in the Revolutionary War. This state is historically nicknamed The Jersey Blue State, after the blue uniforms of its Revolutionary soldiers.

CONNECTICUT

5TH STATE

Connecticut's state bird is the American Robin.

AMERICAN ROBIN

HARTFORD

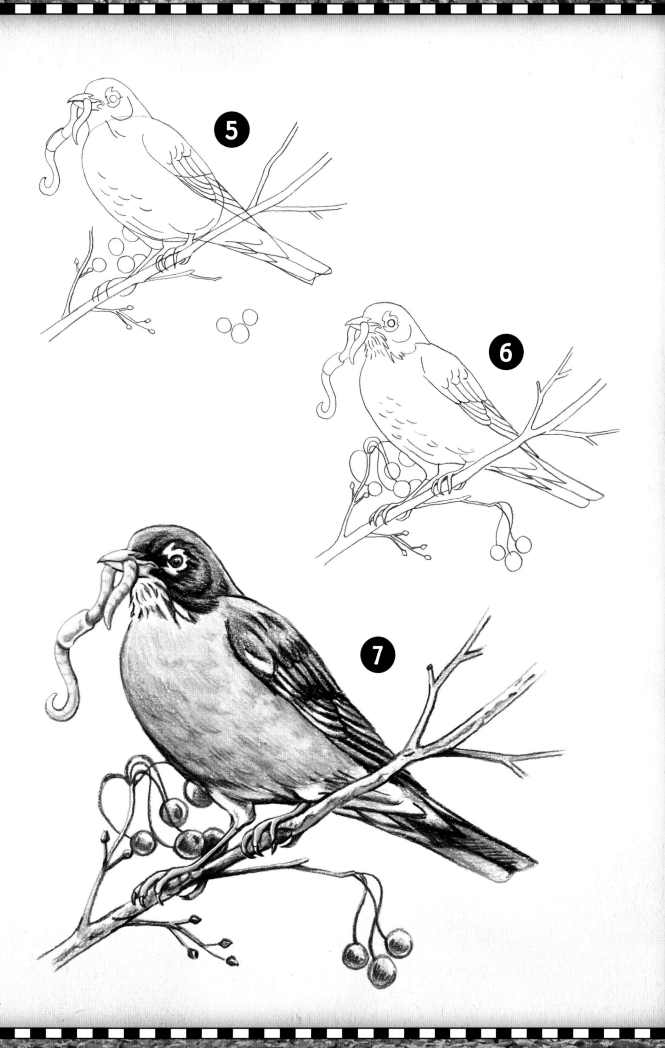

MASSACHUSETTS

6TH STATE

The *Mayflower* set sail from England on September 6, 1620, with 140 people bound for the "New World."

THE MAYFLOWER

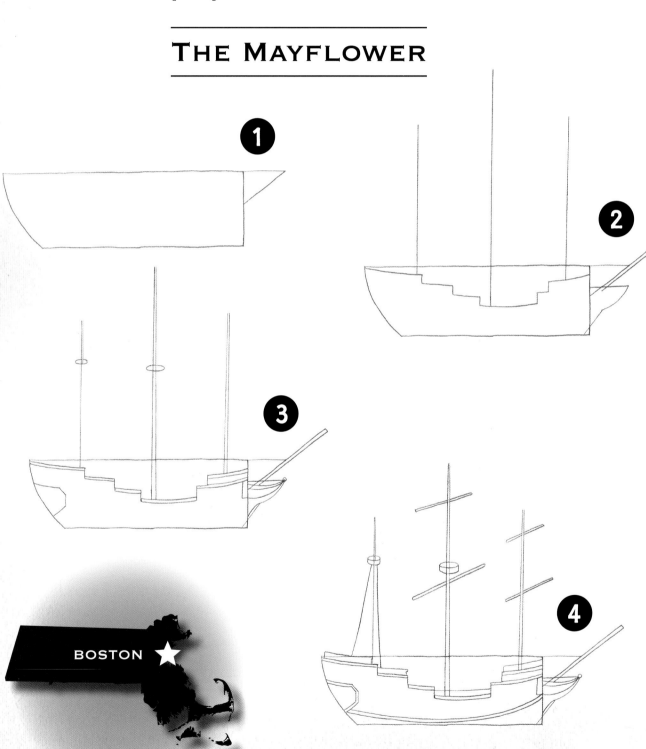

STATE FACT

The *Mayflower* traveled 2,750 miles at an average speed of 2 mph. After more than two months at sea, the ship anchored in what is now Provincetown Harbor on Nov. 11, 1620.

MARYLAND

7TH STATE

Maryland's state bird is the Baltimore Oriole. The city of Baltimore even named its professional baseball team after its feathered friend!

BALTIMORE ORIOLE

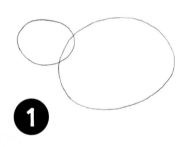

1

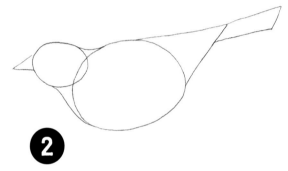

2

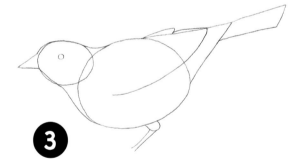

3

ANNAPOLIS ★

4

STATE FACT

During the War of 1812, Fort McHenry was attacked with many weapons, including rockets. Francis Scott Key was so inspired as he watched the successful defense of the fort that he wrote "The Star-Spangled Banner," which is now America's national anthem.

SOUTH CAROLINA

8TH STATE

South Carolina's state flower,
yellow jessamine, is a climbing plant.

YELLOW JESSAMINE

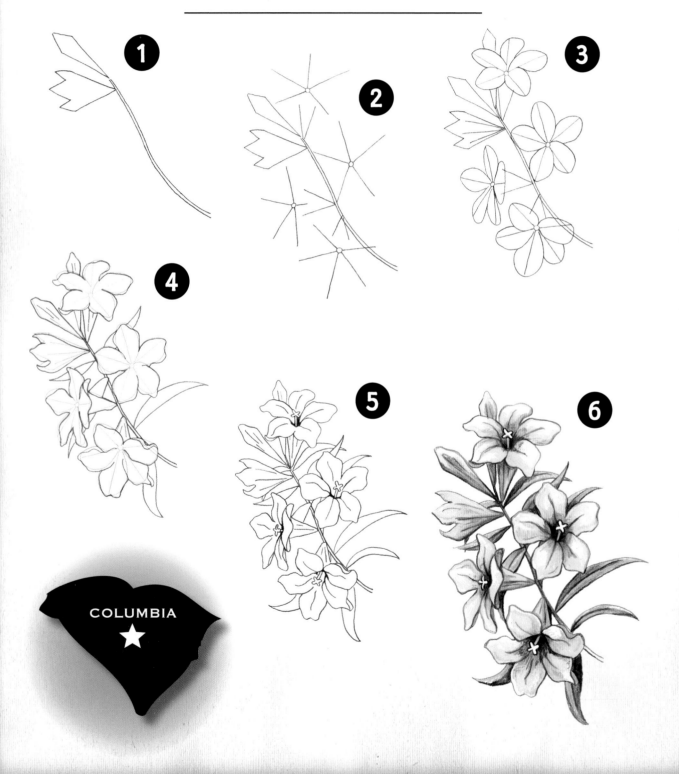

COLUMBIA

NEW HAMPSHIRE

9TH STATE

The state bird of New Hampshire is the purple finch.

PURPLE FINCH

VIRGINIA

1OTH STATE

Pocahontas is remembered for promoting peace between the English colonists and her Powhatan tribe.

POCAHONTAS

RICHMOND

NEW YORK

11TH STATE

The Statue of Liberty was a gift from France to the U.S. in recognition of the friendship between the countries.

STATUE OF LIBERTY

ALBANY

4

5

6

7

EMPIRE STATE BUILDING

1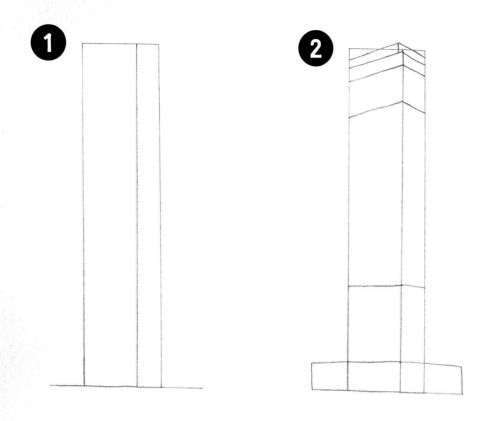

2

3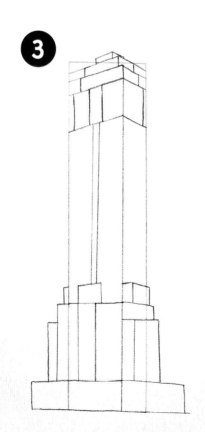

4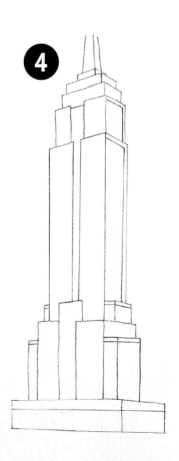

5

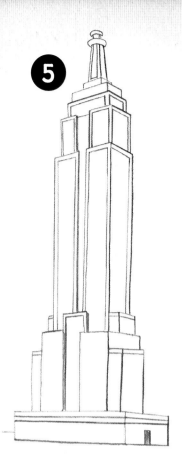

6

7

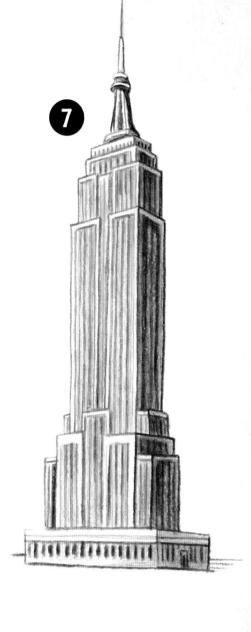

NIAGARA FALLS

Niagara Falls State Park is the oldest state park in the U.S., established in 1885 as the Niagara Reservation.

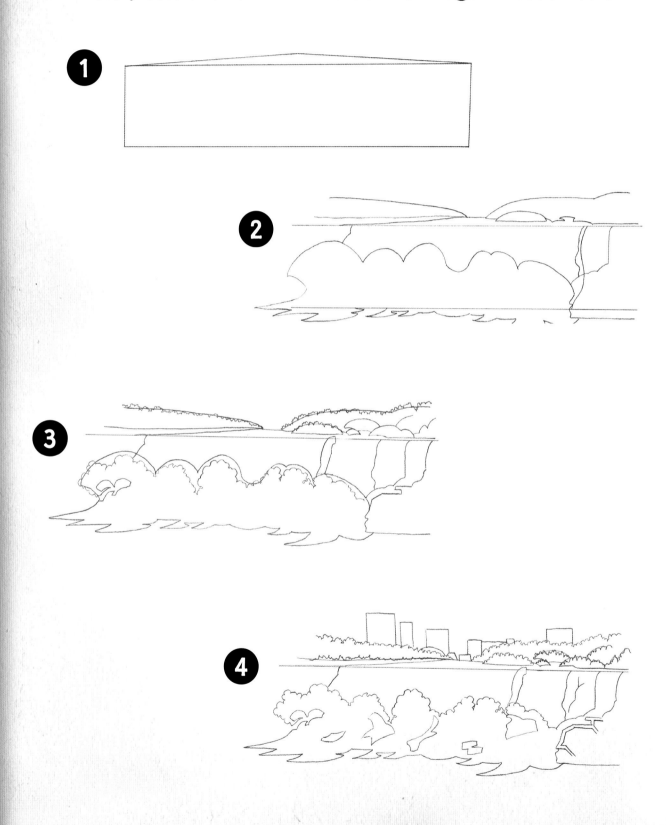

5

6

7

NORTH CAROLINA

12TH STATE

The Wright brothers piloted the first flight in 1903 in Kitty Hawk, North Carolina.

FIRST FLIGHT

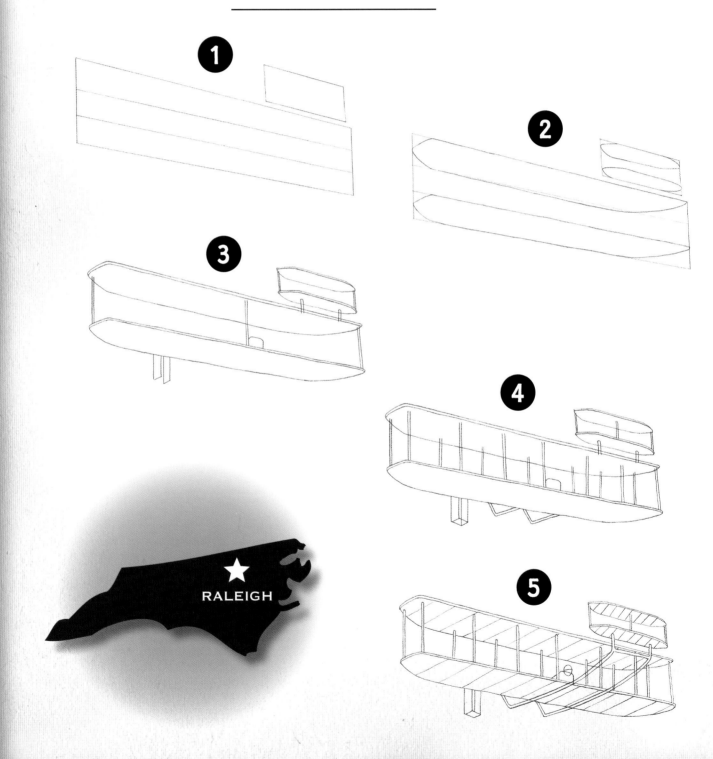

RALEIGH

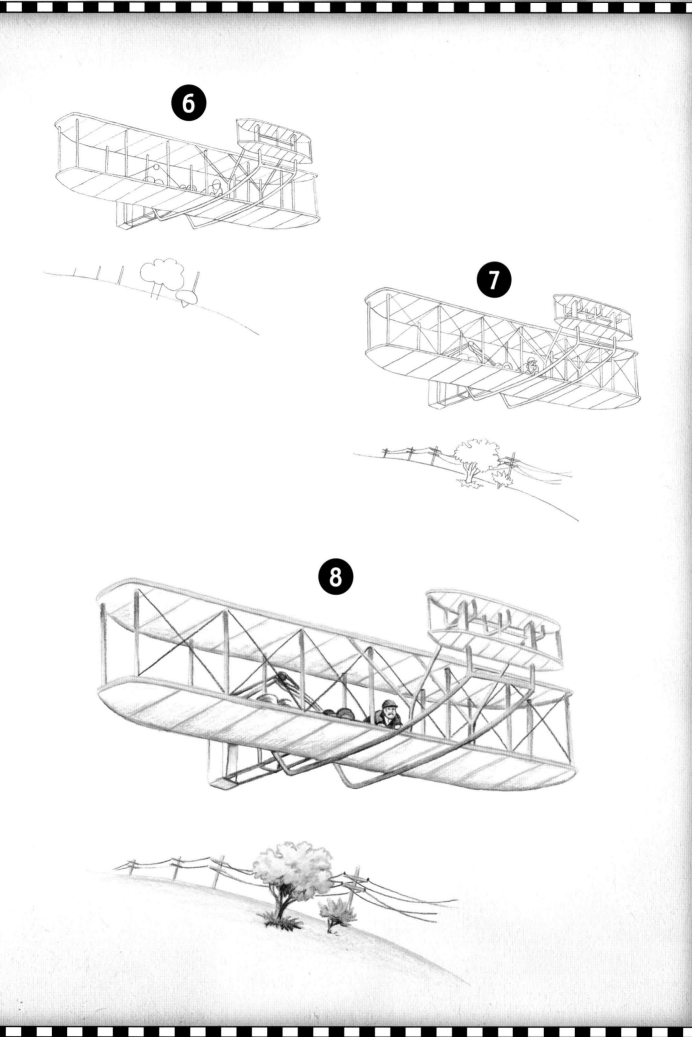

RHODE ISLAND

13TH STATE

One of Rhode Island's nicknames is the "Ocean State."

SAILBOAT

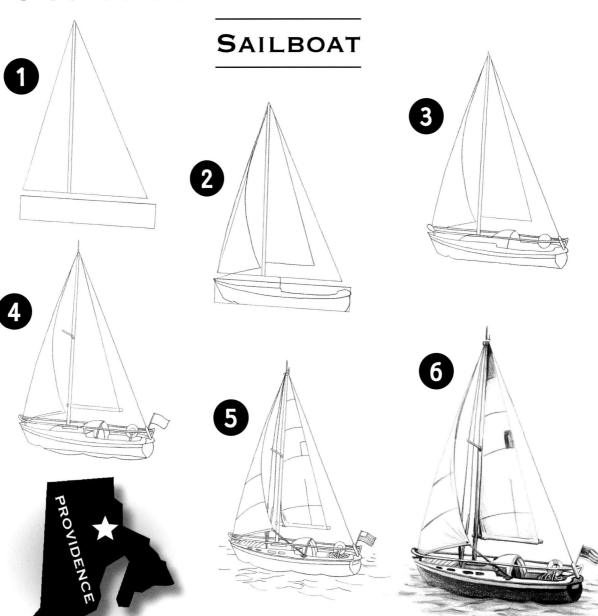

1
2
3
4
5
6

PROVIDENCE

STATE FACT

All Rhode Islanders live within a 30-minute drive to the Atlantic Ocean or the Narragansett Bay. No wonder sailing is the most popular sport in the state!

VERMONT

14TH STATE

Vermont's state tree is the sugar maple.

MAPLE LEAF

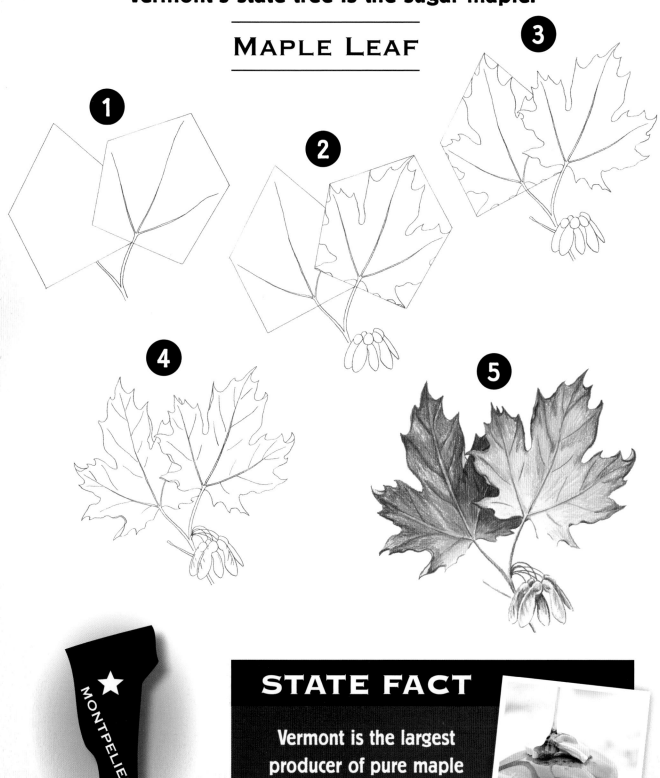

STATE FACT

Vermont is the largest producer of pure maple syrup in the United States.

KENTUCKY

15TH STATE

Daniel Boone founded Boonesborough, the first American settlement in Kentucky.

DANIEL BOONE

FRANKFORT

TENNESSEE

16TH STATE

Music is one of Tennessee's top industries.

GUITAR

1

2

NASHVILLE

3

4

5

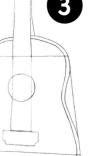

6

STATE FACT

Tennessee's capital, Nashville, has more than 100 music recording studios, and Memphis is known as "Birthplace of the Blues."

MISSISSIPPI

20TH STATE

Mississippi's state flower is the magnolia.

MAGNOLIA

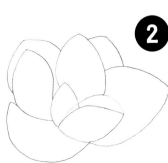

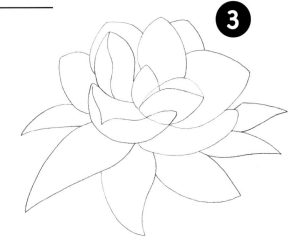

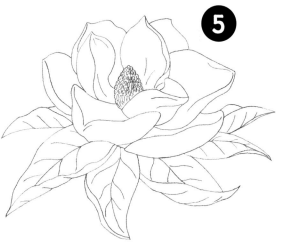

JACKSON

OHIO

17TH STATE

Twenty-five astronauts, including Neil Armstrong, are from Ohio.

BIRTHPLACE OF AVIATION

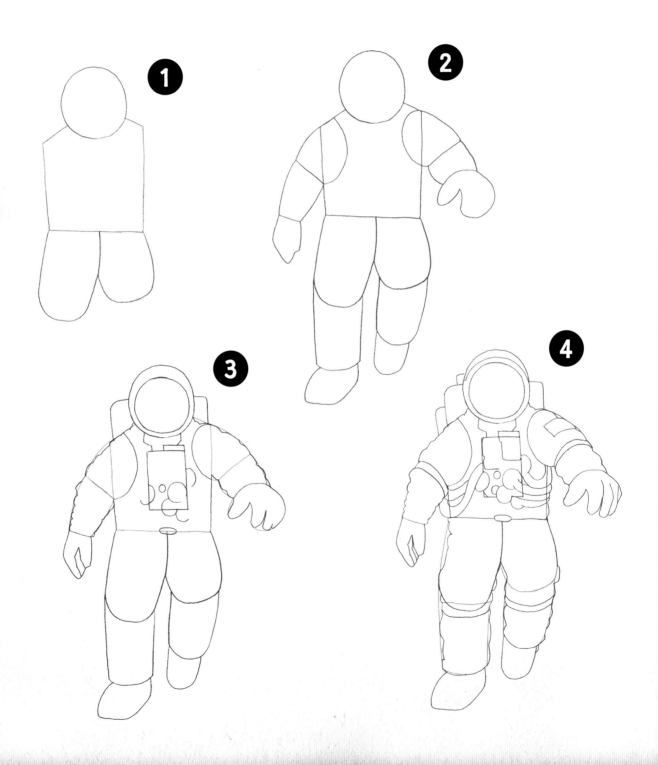

38

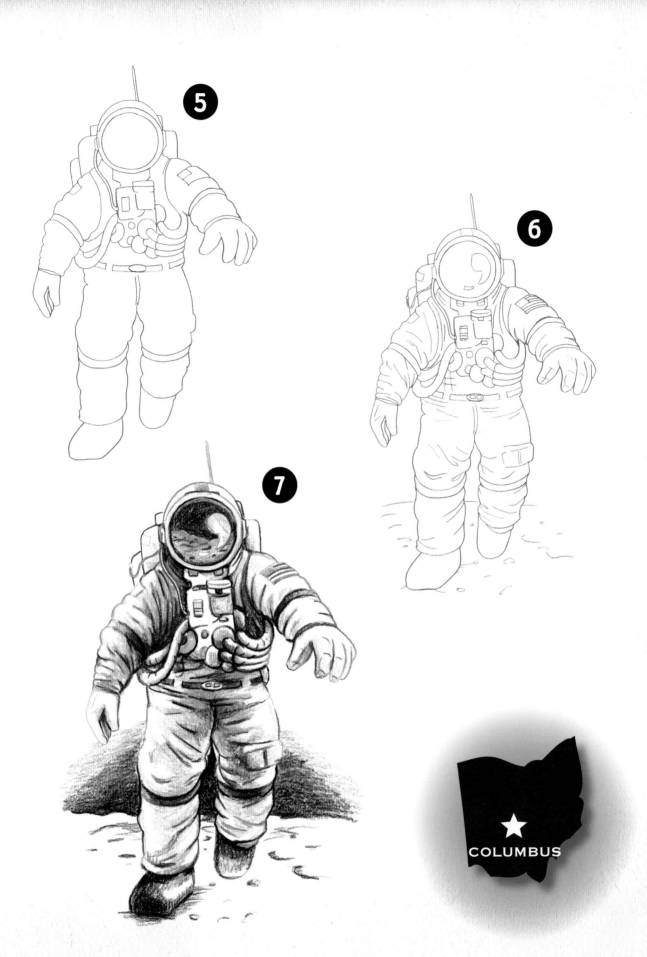

COLUMBUS

LOUISIANA

18TH STATE

Louisiana's state bird is the brown pelican.

BROWN PELICAN

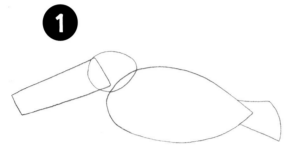

1

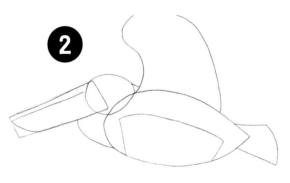

2

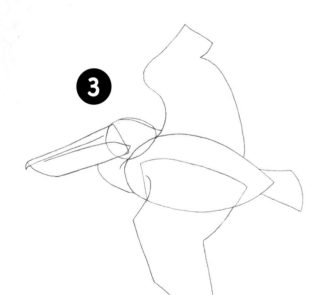

3

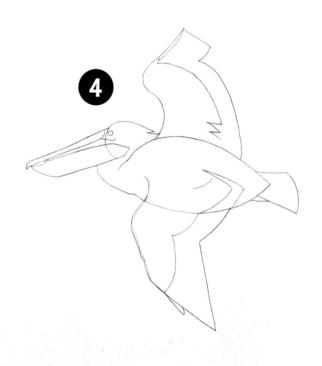

4

BATON ROUGE ★

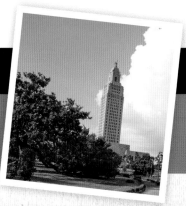

INDIANA

Indianapolis is best known for its speedway motor racing. The Indianapolis 500 is the oldest car race in the world!

INDY RACECAR

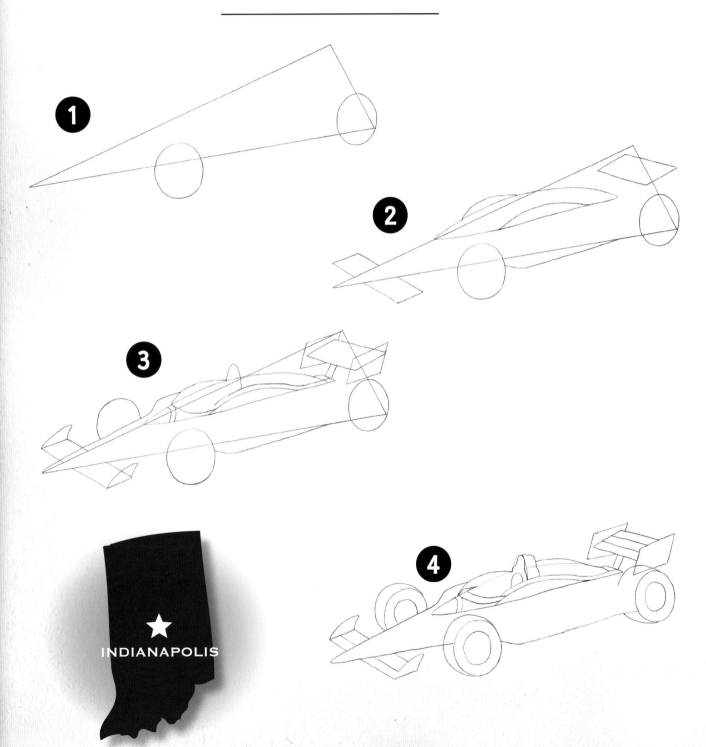

INDIANAPOLIS

5

6

7

STATE FACT

The Indianapolis Motor Speedway is the world's largest spectator sporting facility, with more than 250,000 seats.

43

ILLINOIS

**Formerly called Sears Tower,
this skyscraper stands 110 stories high.**

WILLIS TOWER

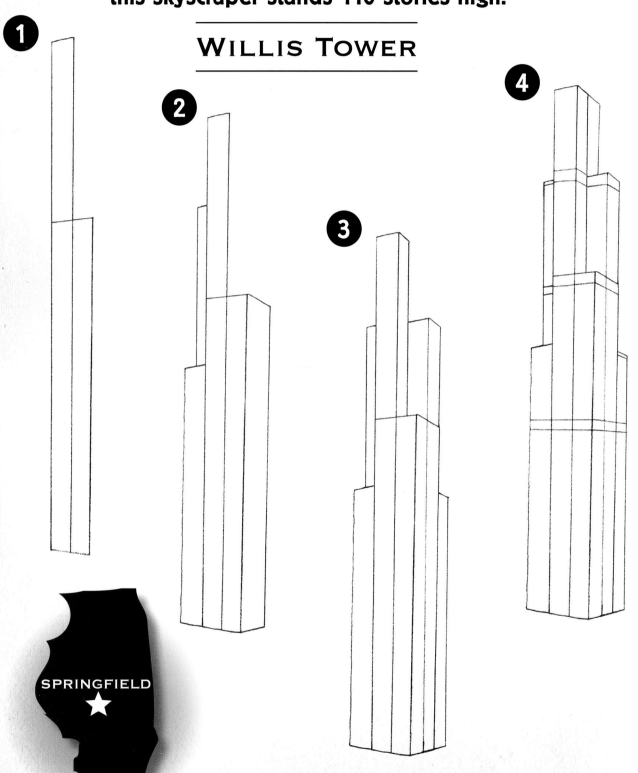

1

2

3

4

SPRINGFIELD
★

44

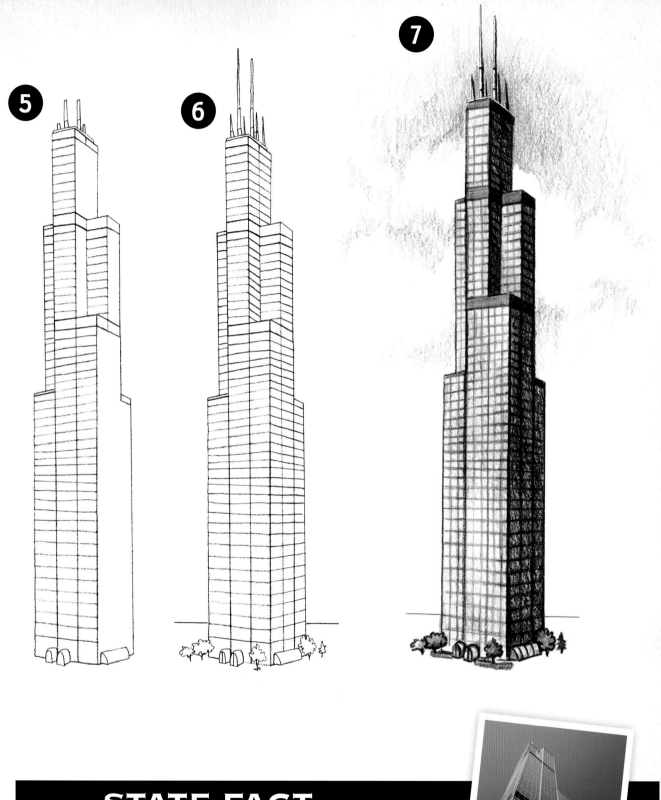

5 **6** **7**

45

ROUTE 66

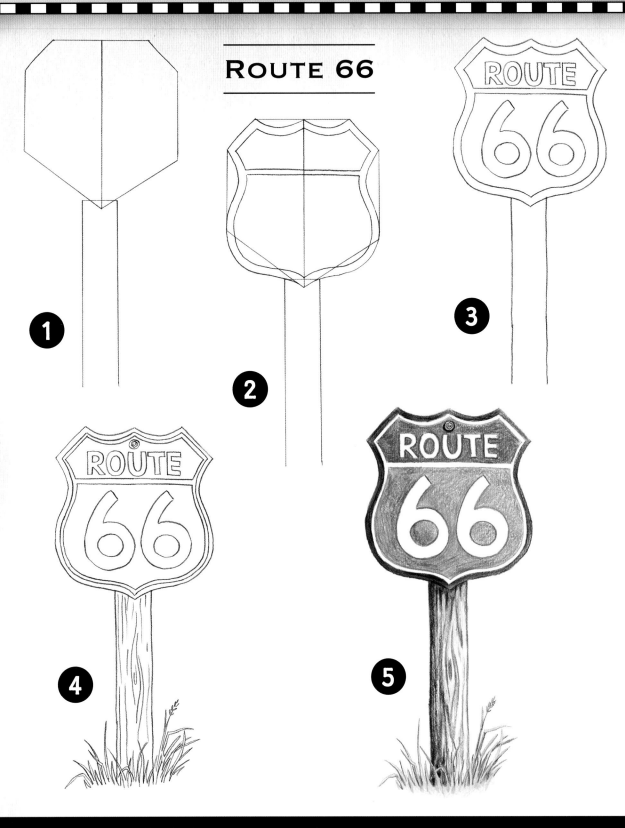

1

2

3

4

5

STATE FACT

Route 66 starts in Illinois and winds through seven other states—Missouri, Kansas, Oklahoma, Texas, New Mexico, Arizona, and California—covering 2,448 miles.

ALABAMA

22ND STATE

Alabama's state bird, the yellowhammer, is a type of woodpecker.

YELLOWHAMMER

The Maine lobster, also known as the American lobster,
is the largest kind of lobster.

MAINE LOBSTER

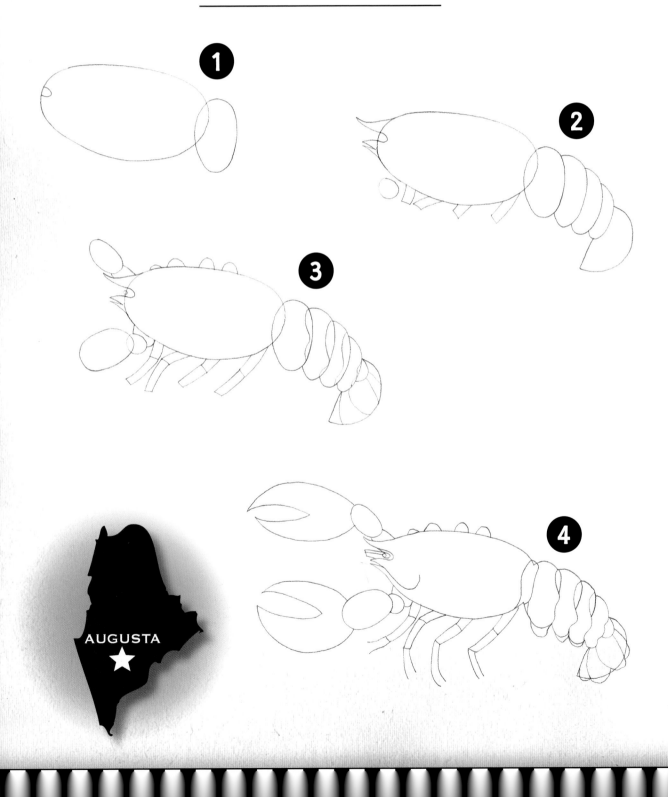

AUGUSTA

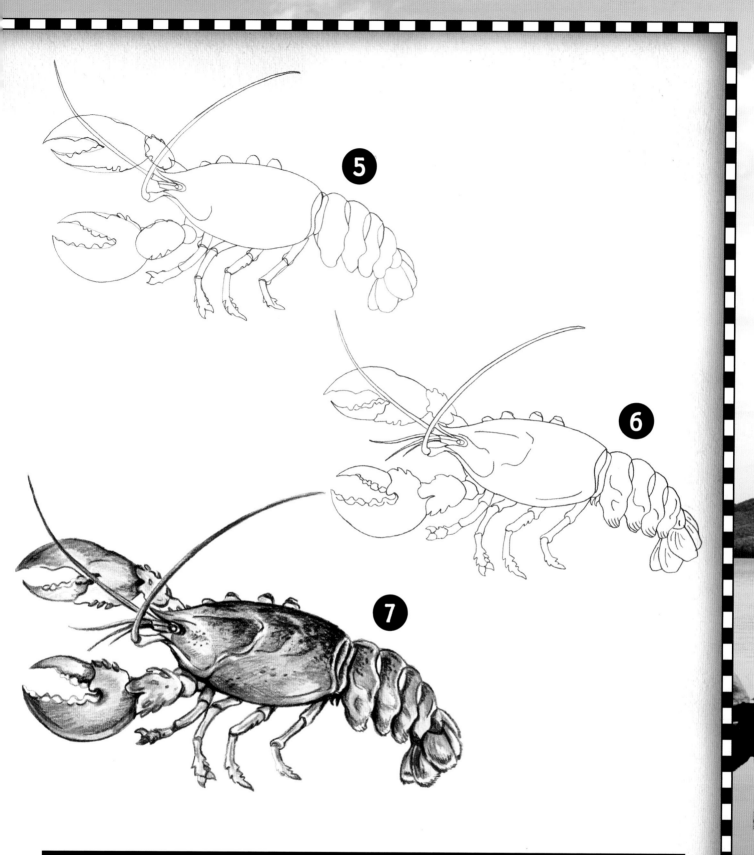

⑤

⑥

⑦

MISSOURI

24TH STATE

The Gateway Arch in St. Louis commemorates the westward expansion of the U.S.

GATEWAY TO THE WEST

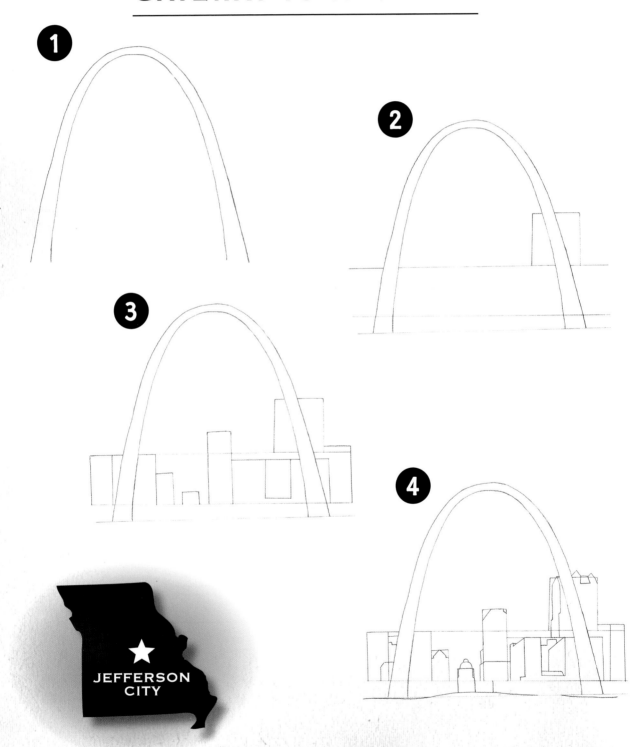

1

2

3

4

JEFFERSON CITY

5

6

7

ARKANSAS

25TH STATE

**Arkansas is known for its razorback hogs,
or wild boars, found in more than 50 counties in the state.**

RAZORBACK HOG

1
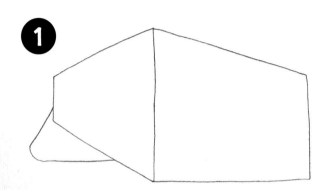

2
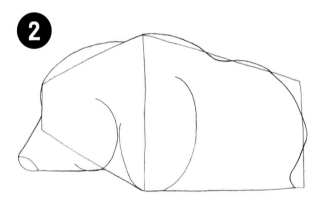

3
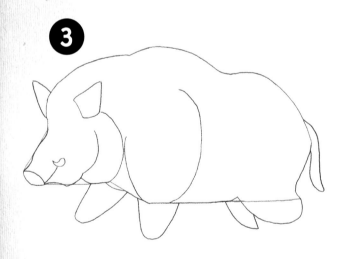

4

★ LITTLE ROCK

5 **6** **7**

MICHIGAN

26TH STATE

Lake Michigan is the only Great Lake that the U.S. doesn't share with Canada.

LAKE MICHIGAN

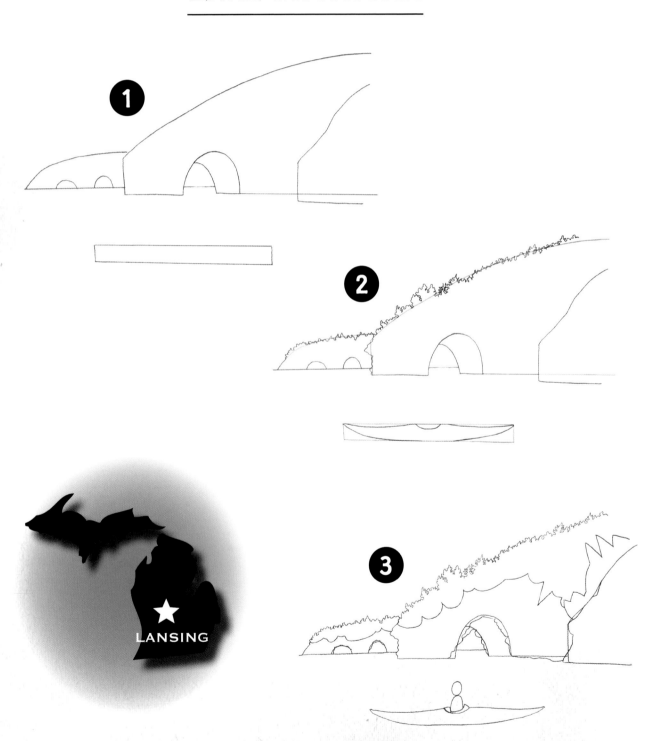

LANSING

FLORIDA

The John F. Kennedy Space Center in Orlando has been the launchpad for every American-manned space mission.

SPACE SHUTTLE

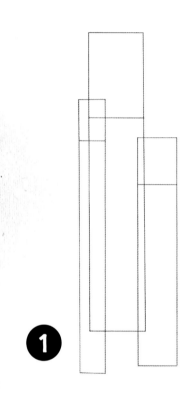

1

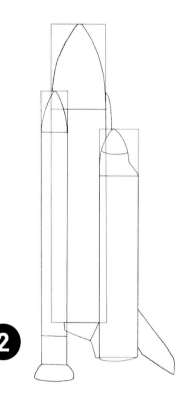

2

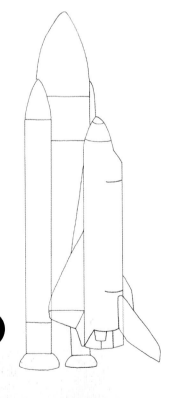

3

TALLAHASSEE

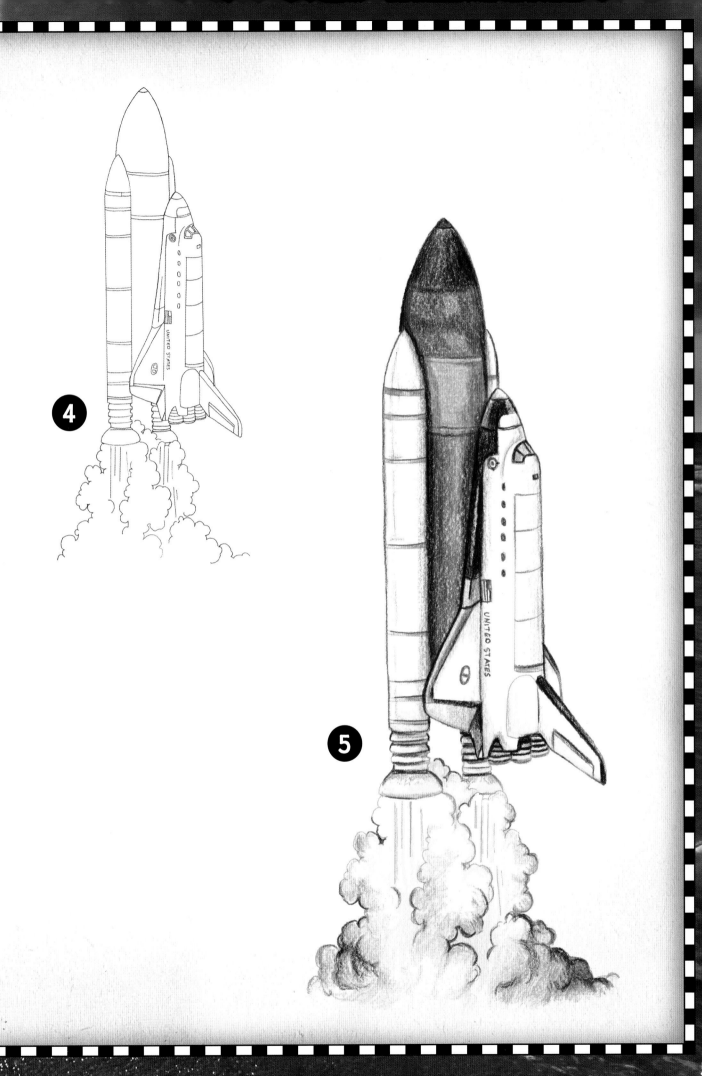

TEXAS

28TH STATE

The Alamo, one of the most well-known monuments in Texas, was the site of much activity during the Texan Revolution.

THE ALAMO

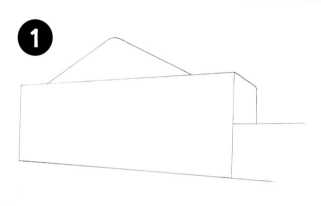

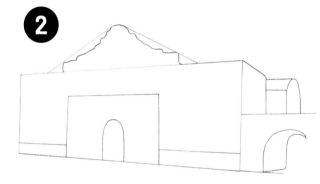

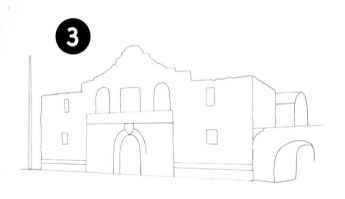

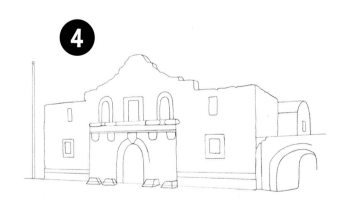

★ AUSTIN

5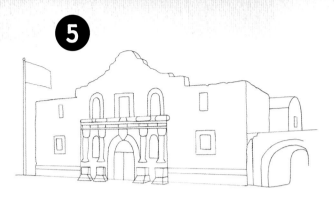

6

7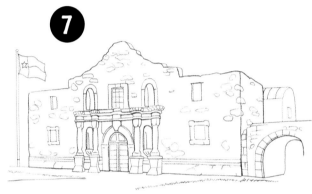

8

IOWA

29TH STATE

Iowa has more than 90,000 farms, many of which grow corn.

THE TALL CORN STATE

1

2

3

4

5

6

★ DES MOINES

7

WISCONSIN

30TH STATE

The World Dairy Expo takes place in Madison each year, attracting more than 70,000 visitors.

THE DAIRY STATE

1

2

3

4

5

6

MADISON

CALIFORNIA

31ST STATE

The Golden Gate Bridge is more than a mile long and spans San Francisco Bay.

THE GOLDEN GATE BRIDGE

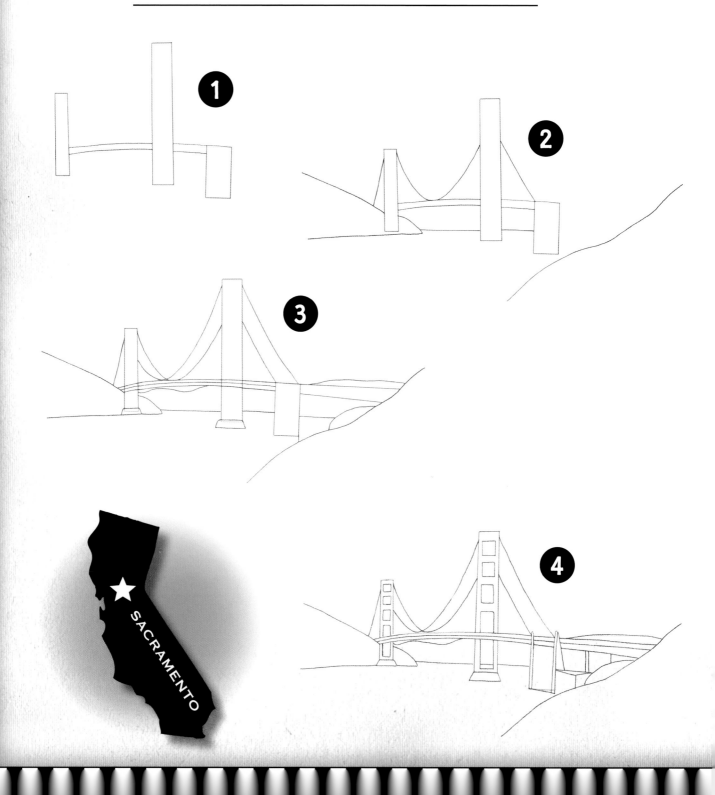

MINNESOTA

32ND STATE

Minnesota's state bird, the common loon, can have a wingspan of up to five feet!

COMMON LOON

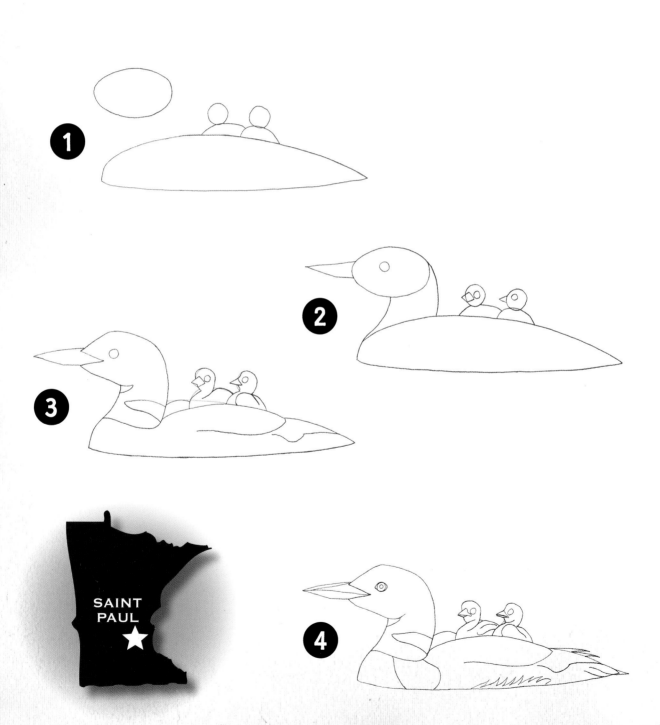

SAINT
PAUL

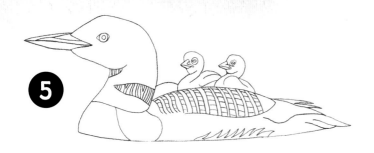

5

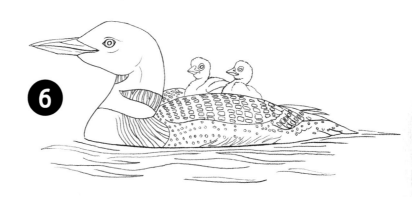

6

7

OREGON

33RD STATE

Crater Lake is a beautiful national park that attracts an average of 482,000 visitors each year.

CRATER LAKE

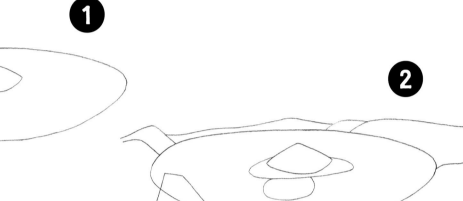

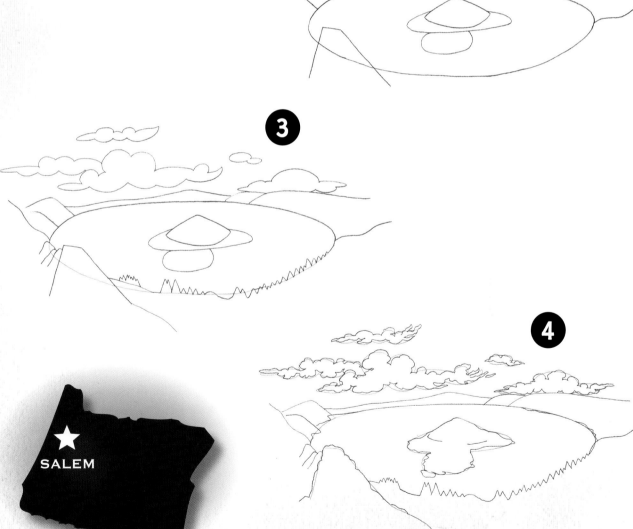

SALEM

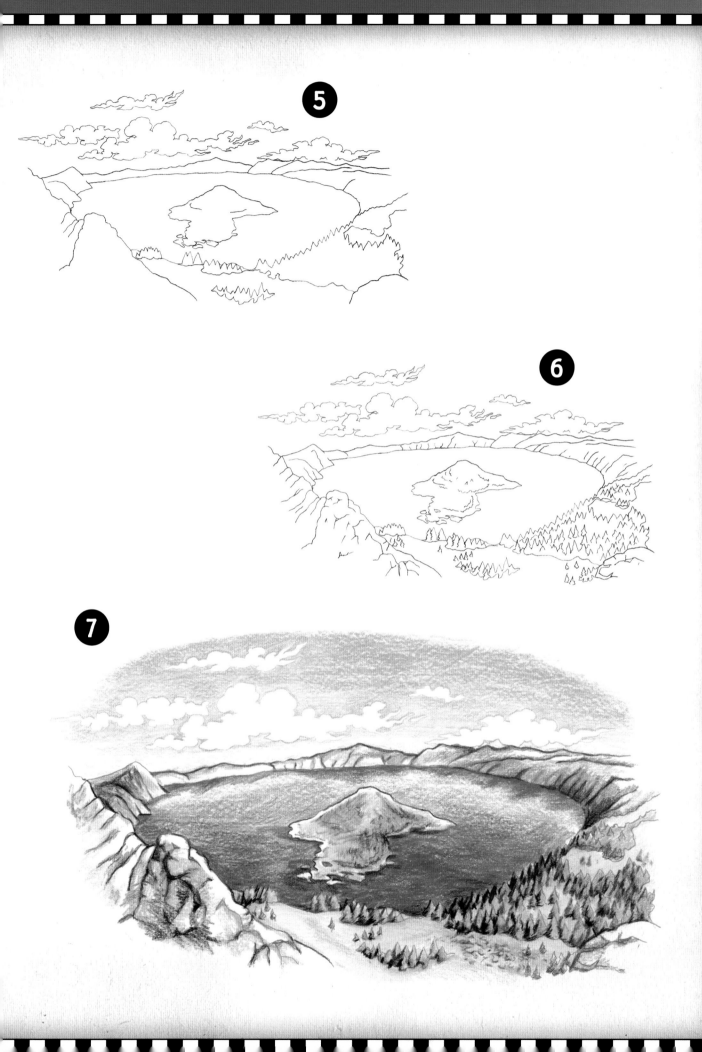

KANSAS

34TH STATE

Kansas is nicknamed the "Sunflower State," after its state flower.

SUNFLOWER

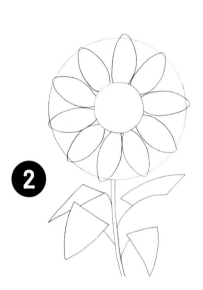

1

2

3

4

5

6

★

TOPEKA

WEST VIRGINIA

35TH STATE

West Virginia's state bird is the cardinal.

CARDINAL

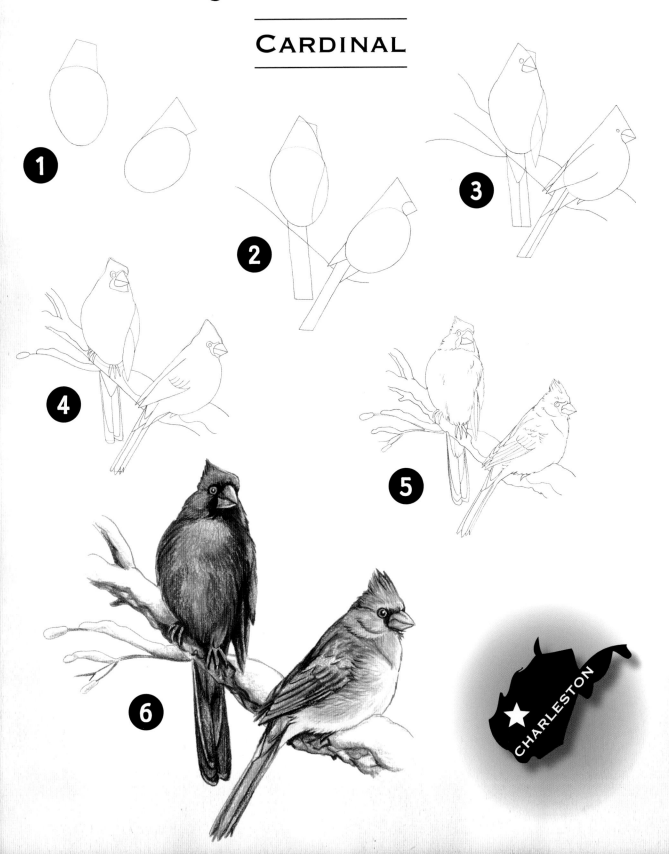

NEVADA

36TH STATE

More than half of the mustangs in the U.S. are located in Nevada.

MUSTANG

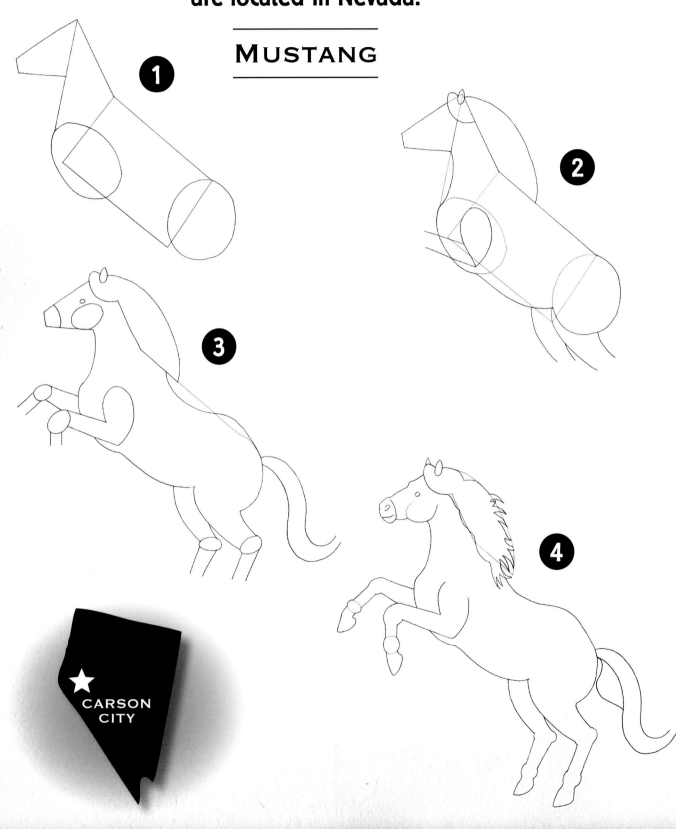

CARSON CITY

5

6

7

STATE FACT

"Mustang" is another word for wild horse. It comes from the Spanish word *mestano,* meaning "ownerless" or "stray horse."

NEBRASKA

37TH STATE

Nebraska was the starting point of the Oregon Trail, which many pioneers followed west to Oregon and California.

COVERED WAGON

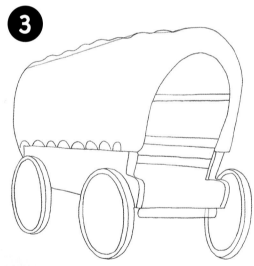

★ LINCOLN

5 **6** **7**

STATE FACT

Pioneer families headed west in the 1800s, transporting their possessions in wagons that were about 10 feet long and 4 feet wide. These wagons were called "prairie schooners" because the canvas cover resembled a ship's sail.

COLORADO

38TH STATE

The Rocky Mountain Bighorn Sheep is Colorado's state animal.

ROCKY MOUNTAIN BIGHORN SHEEP

DENVER

NORTH DAKOTA

39TH STATE

Native Americans in North Dakota and other plains states relied on bison for food, shelter, and clothing.

BISON

SOUTH DAKOTA

40TH STATE

Mount Rushmore National Monument showcases carvings of four presidents: George Washington, Thomas Jefferson, Theodore Roosevelt, and Abraham Lincoln.

MOUNT RUSHMORE

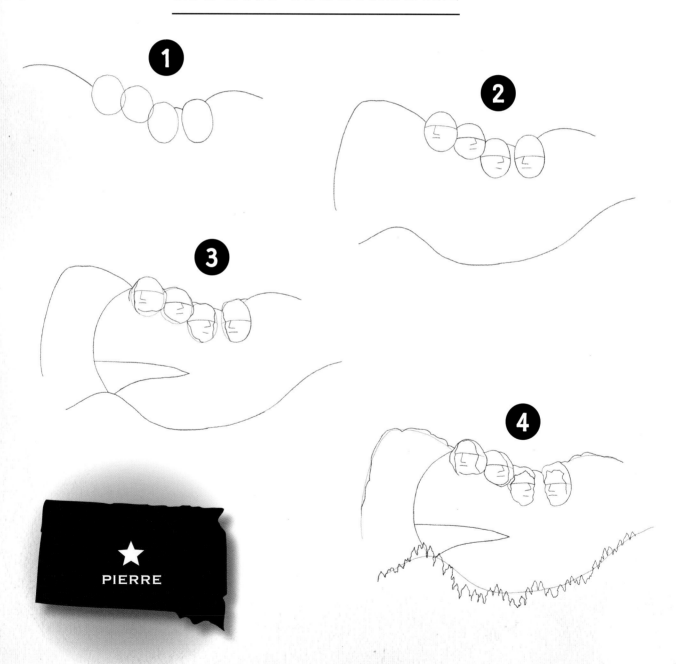

PIERRE

MONTANA

41ST STATE

Crazy Horse is remembered for his role in the Battle of Little Bighorn, also known as Custer's Last Stand.

CRAZY HORSE

1

2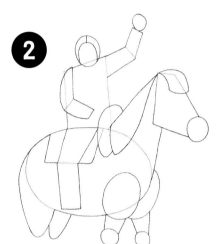

3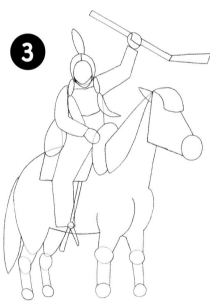

4

HELENA

STATE FACT

The largest snowflake ever observed was recorded in Montana on January 28, 1887, at almost 15 inches wide.

WASHINGTON

42ND STATE

The Space Needle was built in 1962 for the World Fair.

SEATTLE SPACE NEEDLE

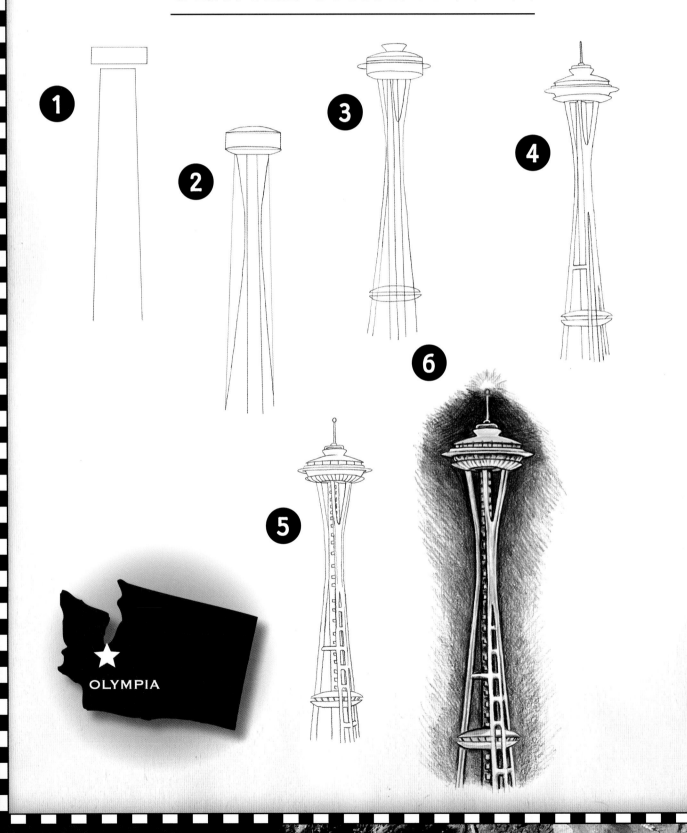

OLYMPIA

KING SALMON

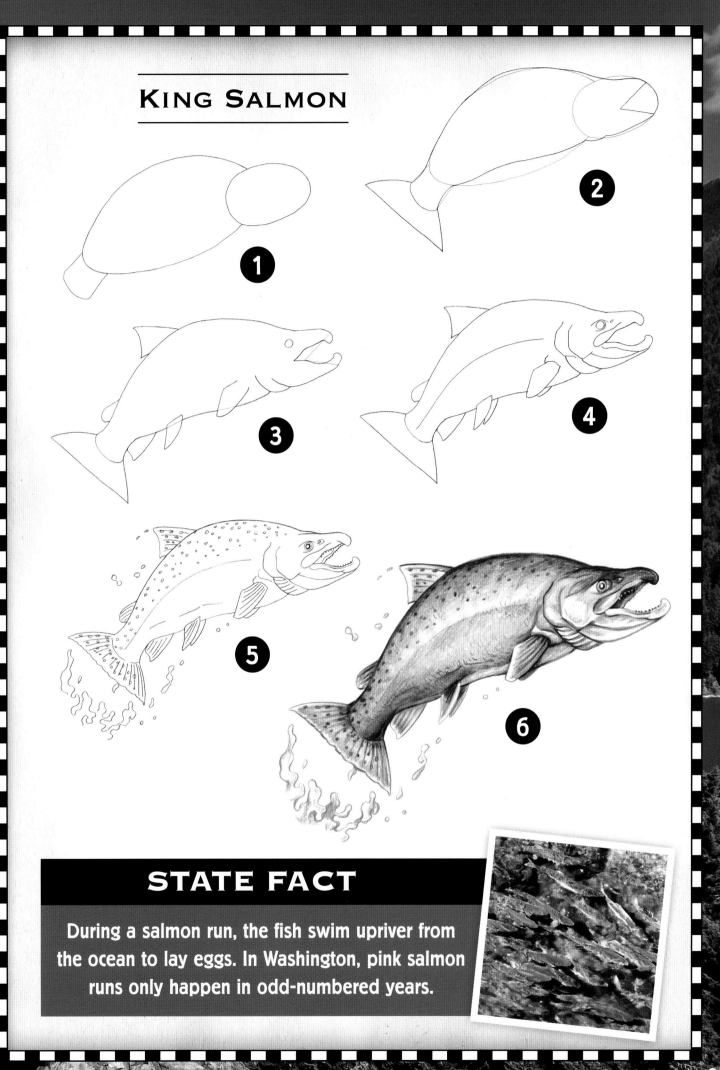

IDAHO

43RD STATE

Many types of important minerals can be found in Idaho, but silver and phosphate are the two major minerals produced in the state.

MINER

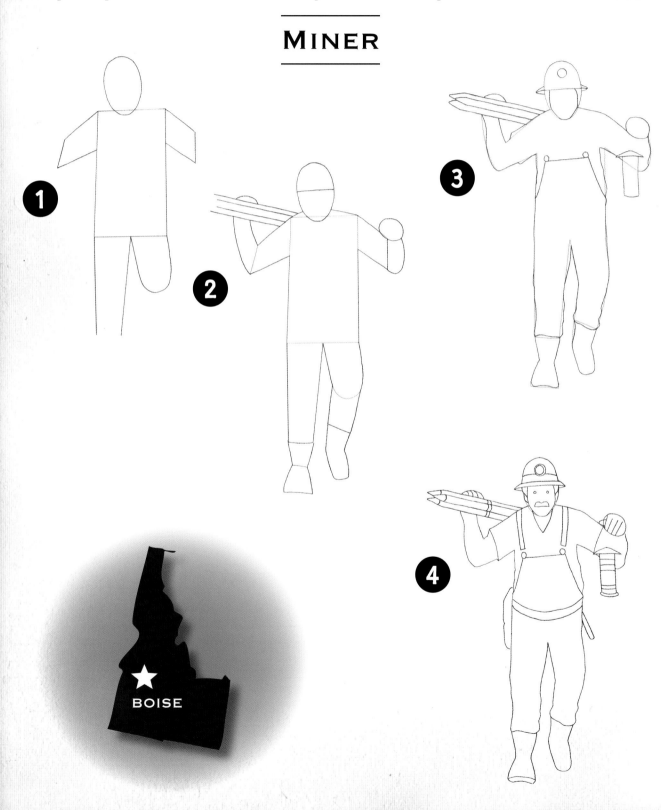

BOISE

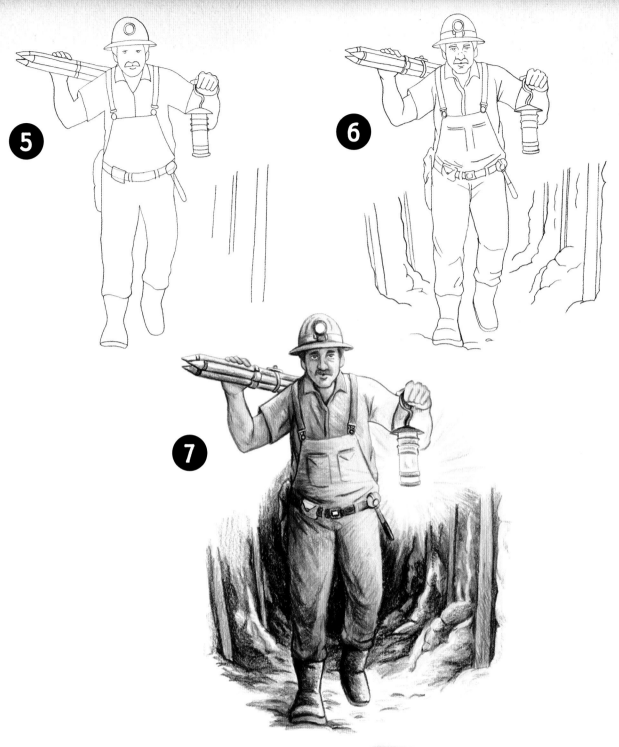

5

6

7

STATE FACT

The Coeur d'Alene mining district in Shoshone County is one of the two richest metal mining areas in the world.

WYOMING

44TH STATE

Old Faithful is a cone geyser in Yellowstone National Park.

OLD FAITHFUL

CHEYENNE

6

STATE FACT

Approximately every 76 minutes,
Old Faithful shoots up to 8,400 gallons of
boiling water 150 feet in the air!

DEVILS TOWER

1

2

3

4

5

FUN FACT

The top of Devils Tower National Monument is about the size of a football field.

OKLAHOMA

46TH STATE

Oklahoma had 13 different flags between 1907 and 1925, when this one was adopted.

STATE FLAG

 1
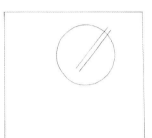

2

3

4

5
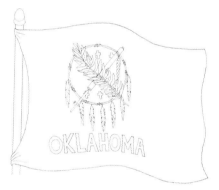

6

OKLAHOMA CITY ★

STATE FACT

Oklahoma's flag design honors more than 60 groups of Native Americans and their ancestors, including the Choctaw and Osage tribes.

UTAH

45TH STATE

Utah is known as the "Crossroads of the West" because its railroads were important in the development of the American West.

STEAM LOCOMOTIVE

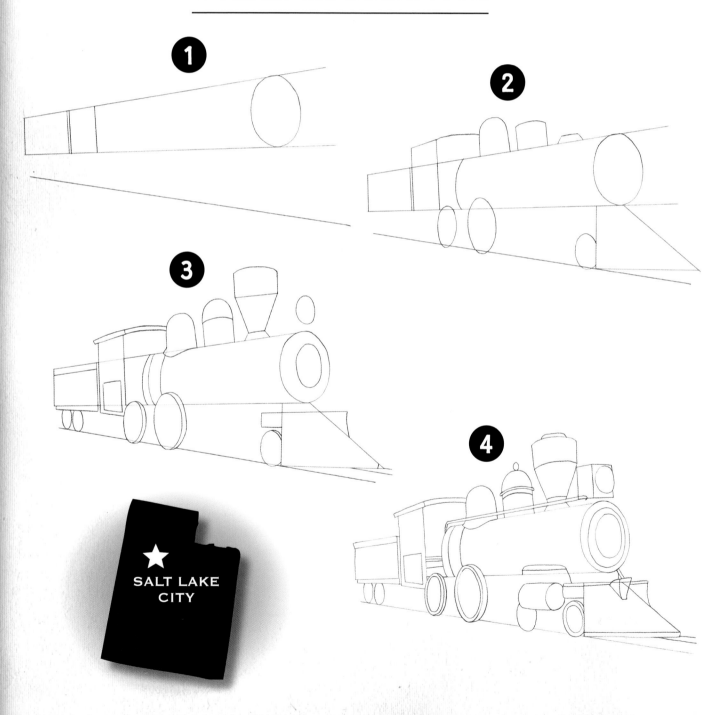

SALT LAKE
CITY

STATE FACT

Utah was making history before it was even a
state. The world's first transcontinental railroad was
completed at Promontory, where the Central Pacific
and Union Pacific Railroads met, on May 10, 1869.
Today the spot is a U.S. National Historic Site.

NEW MEXICO

47TH STATE

The Albuquerque Balloon Fiesta occurs every October—it's the most photographed event in the world!

HOT AIR BALLOON

SANTA FE

ARIZONA

48TH STATE

**The saguaro cactus is the state flower of Arizona.
It blooms in May and June.**

SAGUARO CACTUS

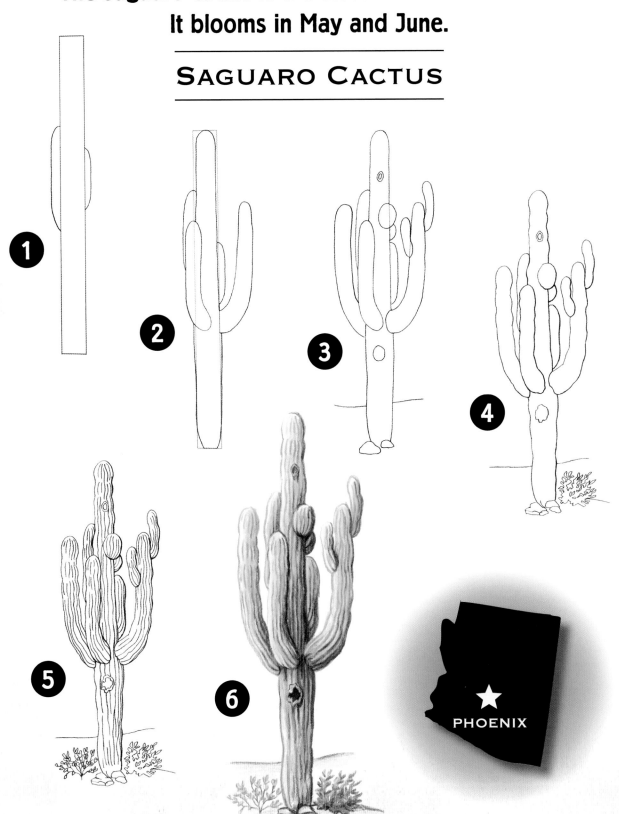

PHOENIX

ALASKA

49TH STATE

Alaska is often referred to as "Bear Country." All three species of North American bears live in Alaska, including the grizzly.

GRIZZLY BEAR

JUNEAU ★

5

6

STATE FACT

Glaciers cover about 5 percent of Alaska. Nearly half of the world's active glaciers are found in this big state.

HAWAII

King Kamehameha I unified the Hawaiian Islands in 1810.

KING KAMEHAMEHA I

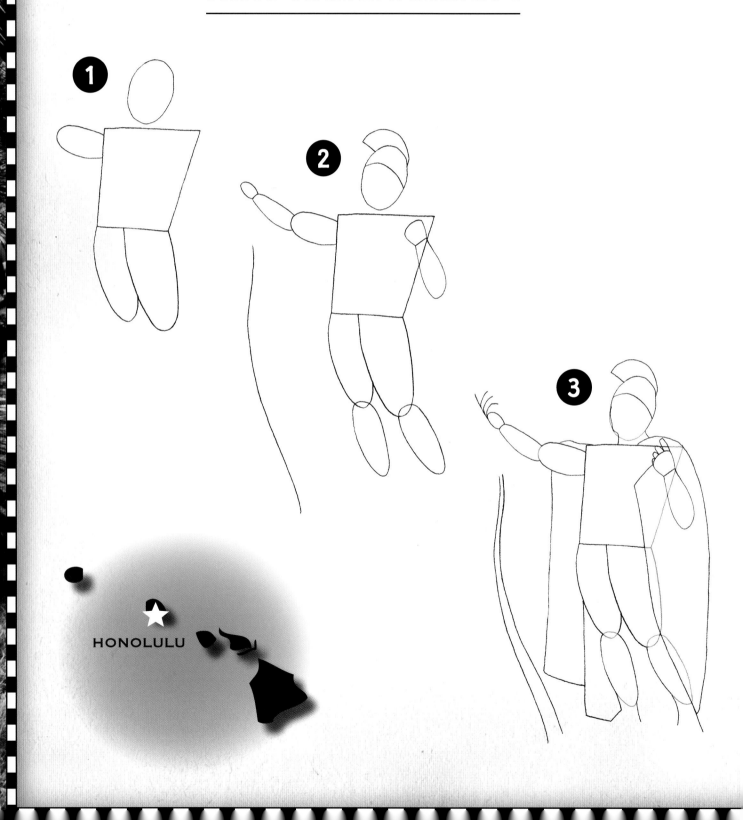

HONOLULU

WASHINGTON, D.C.

Washington, D.C., or the District of Columbia, is the capital of the United States. President George Washington chose the area, as well as the future site of the White House.

THE WHITE HOUSE

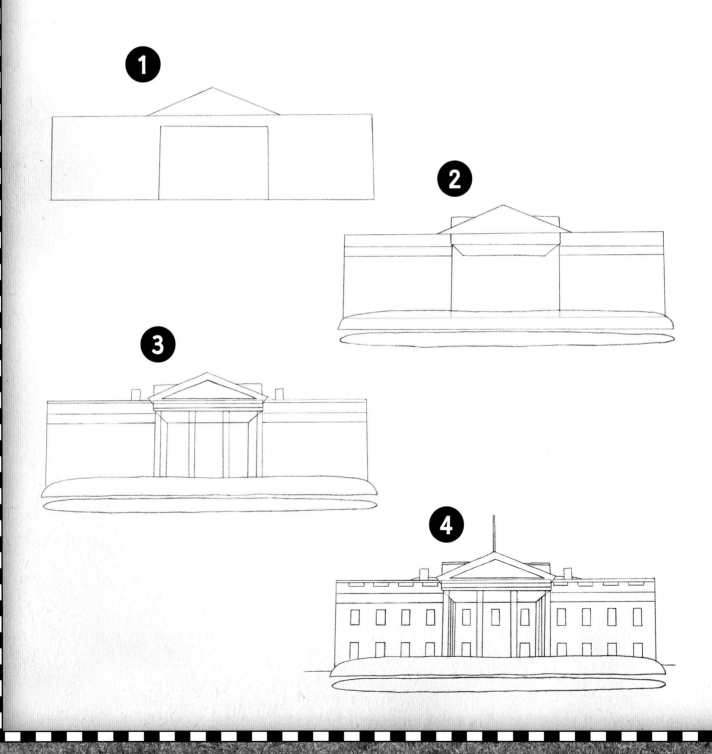

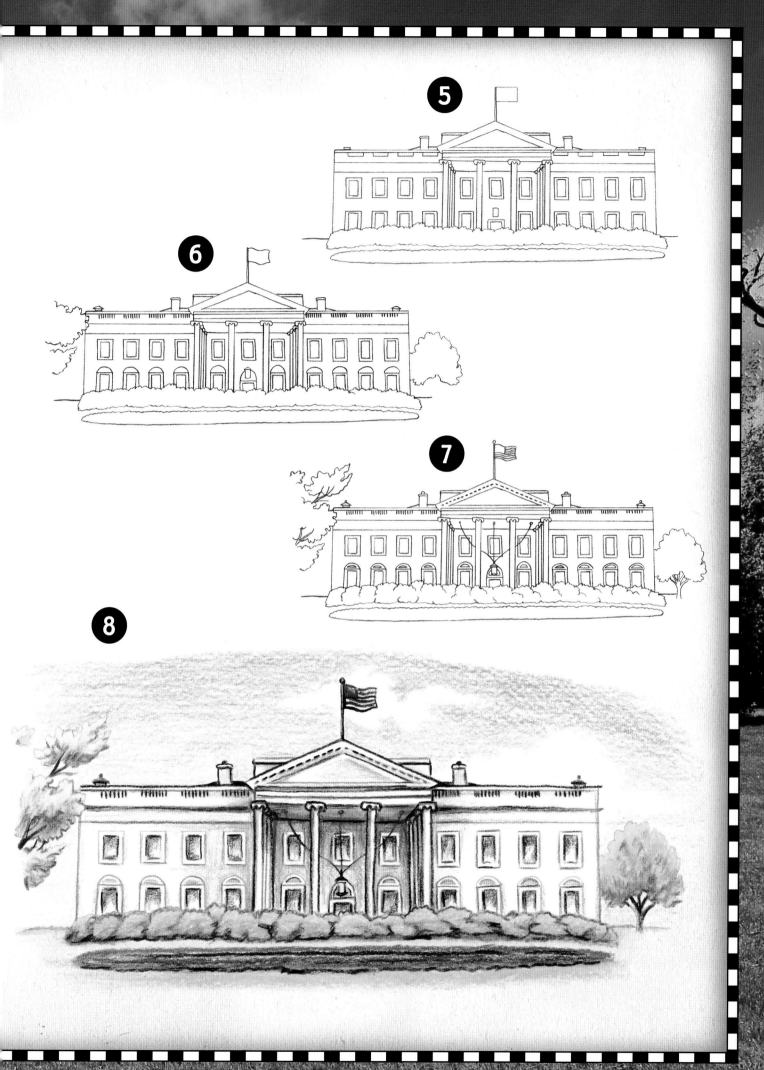

WASHINGTON NATIONAL MONUMENT

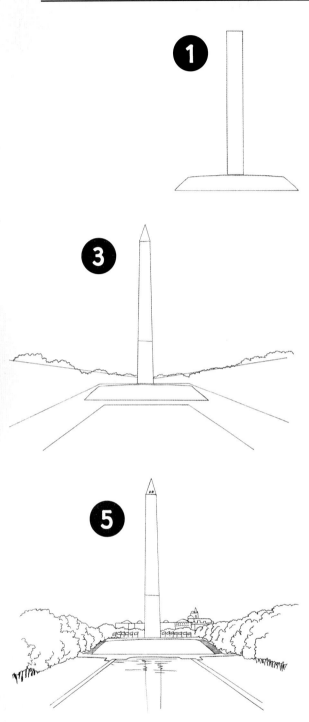

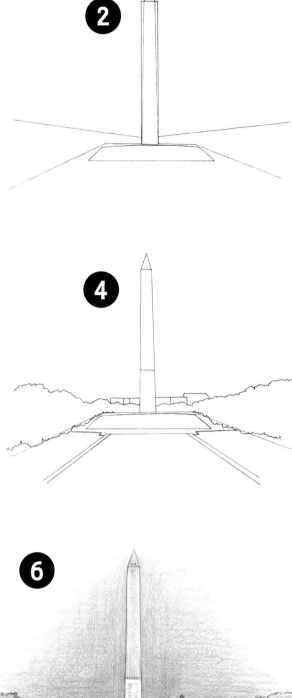

FUN FACT

The Washington National Monument is 555 feet tall!

UNCLE SAM

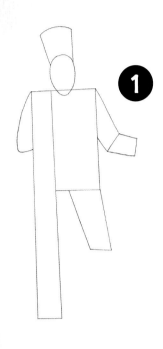

FUN FACT

Uncle Sam is not a real person. In 1930, political cartoonists drew the character as a representation for the nickname given to the United States during the War of 1812. Uncle Sam became an official American symbol in 1961!

BALD EAGLE

5

6

7

FUN FACT

In 1782 the bald eagle was chosen as the emblem of the United States because of its long life, strength, and majestic appearance.

GEORGE WASHINGTON

George Washington was the very first president of the United States of America.

1

2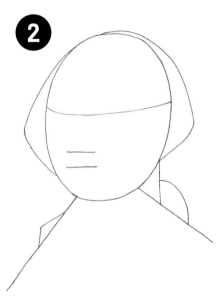

3

4

FUN FACT

When he was 57 years old, George Washington had all his teeth pulled out!

ABRAHAM LINCOLN

Abraham Lincoln was the 16th president of the United States. He led the nation through The Civil War.

FUN FACT

Abraham Lincoln was the tallest U.S. president at 6 feet 4 inches.

PAUL REVERE

Paul Revere is famous for his midnight ride during the Revolutionary War from Boston to Lexington, Massachusetts, to warn that the British were approaching.

PATRICK HENRY

Patrick Henry was a well-known, passionate Virginia politician and speaker who protested British tyranny. Today he is remembered as a symbol of America's struggle for liberty and for his famous words, "Give me liberty, or give me death!"

FUN FACT

Patrick Henry was the first governor of Virginia and led the fight for the adoption of the Bill of Rights, which makes up the first 10 amendments of the U.S. Constitution.

5

6

7

BENJAMIN FRANKLIN

Benjamin Franklin is considered one of the greatest Americans. He was an important statesman, as well as a printer, inventor, librarian, and writer!

THE END

This may be the end of your drawing adventure for now, but you've only explored a few of the places, people, and symbols that make the United States of America special. You can visit your local library to check out books on other American landmarks and historical heroes. With the drawing secrets you've learned, you're all set to create your own drawings of other famous Americans, state birds and flags, and monuments. You can draw Thomas Jefferson, a Native American tepee, Davy Crockett, a California redwood tree, Amelia Earhart, the Grand Canyon, and so much more. With the skills you've learned, the possibilities are endless—all you need is a pencil, paper, and your imagination!

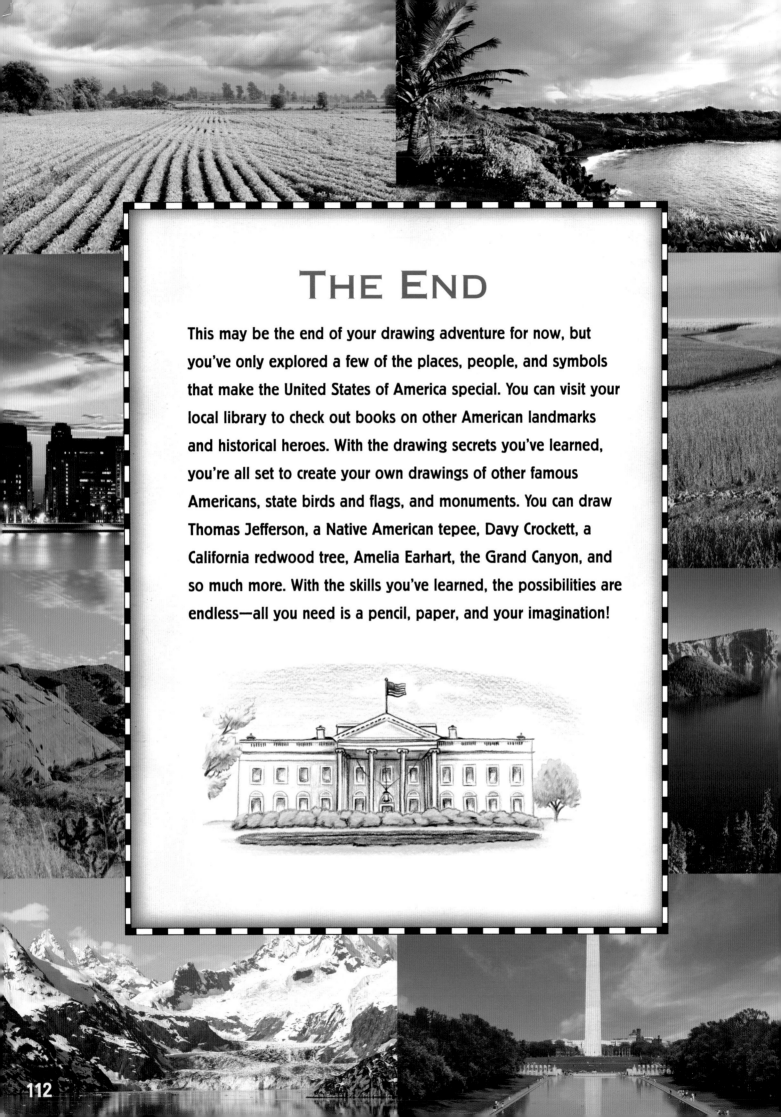